Copyright © 2017 by Eligah Boykin. 771031

ISBN: Softcover   978-1-5434-6911-0
          Hardcover   978-1-5434-6912-7
          EBook   978-1-5434-6910-3

Print information available on the last page

Rev. date: 11/30/2017

To order additional copies of this book, contact:
Xlibris
1-888-795-4274
www.Xlibris.com
Orders@Xlibris.com

DEDICATED
TO
THE MEMORY
OF
PIERRE JAMES RENER

FOREWORD

Here is a tale of High Adventure.

I first penned this script profiting from the mentorship and collaboration of my homeroom, drama and humanities teacher, Pierre James Rener. I believe the 'staff of truth' concept was originally his idea. You could easily consider that it harkens back to a few of those scenes in DeMille's THE TEN COMMANDMENTS. You would not be far off the mark. The ingenuity of the hero may cause you to recall Anansi the Spiderman. That was my sole idea. At that time, the notion of a hero gaining the courage, skill and the spiritual strength to rise above the oppression and exploitation causing his people great suffering was something new to Children's Theater.

This script did well as a children's play touring the inner city and the outer-lying suburbs of Detroit. Professor Rener and his family even went so far as to design and sew the costumes we were to wear for each and every performance. The costumes were so vividly colored we were able to create an atmosphere that made one think of Ishangl Razak, and his talented family of African Drummers and Dancers. What we lacked in fact and authenticity we more than made up for in youthful energy and passion.

Now and again, Professor Rener would suggest I turn this children's play into a book for children. Perhaps he was hoping to help me graduate my creative imagination out of the influence of the heave-ho and chop-socky of muscle men and martial arts movies and the faux African references of Tarzan cinema. One thing is certain, however, it was great to create and celebrate a hero of my own invention. After the tweaking and pruning of many rehearsals and hundreds of performances of this story, you now can discover the adventures of Themba for yourself between the covers of this book.

Now stamp the Staff of Truth three times and close your eyes…

THEMBA AND THE GREAT LION

There were voices in my village that did not come from my mother and my father. These voices did not come from my sisters and brothers, or our friends and neighbors who lived in our village with us. The voices that I speak of did not come from living tongues. These were the voices that came from mothers and fathers, sisters and brothers, as well as friends and neighbors who lived and died long before we were born.

The voices I speak of came from our ancestors.

Our ancestors spoke to us in times of trouble. Whenever any of us were in any danger of being hurt or killed, you could hear their voices everywhere in the land. Sometimes you could hear them speaking in the ground. There were other times when you could hear them speaking in the rocks. Every now and then, you could hear them speaking in the windswept grass and the very trees themselves.

Our ancestors always spoke to us whenever we were in any kind of danger and would advise us what to do.

The Water People were also known to speak to us. The Water People lived in the river Sankuru. The river Sankuru went through to the west of our village, where our mothers washed our clothes. The Water People were able to live in the river Sankuru because they did not have bodies like real people.

These beings were invisible and lived like the spirits in heaven. They were known to tell the river how to flow. The Water People told the clouds when to water our crops, and when this was done, were the ones who painted rainbows across the sky.

We were taught these things when I was very young, among other lessons by the village elders. I was taught these lessons in order to understand why things are as they are today.

The father of heaven, Olurun, would have them this way. The voices of our ancestors, the voices of the Water People, speak and are heard by us because he wills it to be. I learned how to know when these voices were speaking because of his will. I came also to understand what they were saying because of his will. Our elders would have us study carefully and there was much we needed to practice. Nevertheless, as I came to manhood, Olurun willed me understanding that rewarded my years.

Now there were voices in my village that the people could not hear or understand all by themselves. These were the voices of our mightiest spirits and the voices of our gods. The voices of our greatest village heroes were also in this class. The people in my village could not hear and understand these voices, because they came from a special place in heaven. That special place in heaven is known as The Great Time. This is the place where our gods and heroes live forever.

Who could help us to hear and understand the voices of our gods and heroes? There was such a one who could open the invisible door to The Great Time. Bala was his name, and he was The Drummer of the Talking Drum.

Olurun blessed Bala with the gift to hear and speak in special ways. He could hear with his entire body as well as his ears. He could speak the truth of the voices through his soul as well as through his lips. The Drummer of the talking Drum who came before Bala found this to be true. Katanga was his name, and before he died he taught to Bala the entire history of our village by word of mouth.

Katanga taught Bala this, so that the stories and the great deeds of our people would always be remembered. The words of our mightiest spirits would echo and live through Bala's words. The voices of our greatest village heroes would echo through Bala's voice and speak.

The history of our people, when spoken by Bala, would be the magic words to open the invisible door to The Great Time.

So in this way, Bala would speak to us of the sayings and the doings of our most honored spirits, whenever we found the will of Olurun hard to follow. We would find in the stories of our gods and heroes, the wisdom to live as they were known to have lived, with courage and strength.

Bala would pound on the Talking Drum, and the stories he told of our gods and heroes were many.

When the struggles of Life became hard to bear these stories would be told to our people. Times without end, in order to follow the will of Olurun, our people discovered there were great hardships to be overcome.

There was one story that Bala would tell that I was taught. This is the story of Themba and the Great Lion. He told it often to give our people hope. The entire village would gather around Bala when he told this story. I remembered he would tell it in this way-

> "Brothers and sisters, we are here by the will and the grace of Olurun,
> the father of heaven. It is his will that you should hear this story. The
> story of Themba and the Great Lion!
> I am Bala
> Drummer of the Talking Drum
> I will tell this story
> and you will understand-"

Here, the people in my village would chant, "We will understand by the grace of our father in heaven, Olurun."

"You will understand," continued Bala, "that this was once the Kingdom of the Great Lion, Sihkulumi,

    Sihkulumi,

    Sihkulumi,

    Mighty Invader from the land beyond the hills–"

All the villagers would echo, "Mighty Invader from the land beyond the hills!"

"From the land beyond the hills he came, half man and half beast. All fell before before Sihkulumi's mighty roar. He declared himself king, and no one dared to say no–"

So we all shouted, "No one dared to say no!"

Bala's eyes burned like two torches in a very dark cave. "No one dared to say no! From the first moment of his mighty roar, the people lived in TERROR,

                       MISERY,

                            AND SORROW!"

Here we all shouted to the top of our lungs, "TERROR! MISERY! SORROW!"

The rumble of the Talking Drum made our hearts pound, as Bala cried, "TERROR, MISERY, and SORROW that caused many to cry out, to cry out in pain. Among them was Sisiwe, the beautiful wife of Themba, and Mother Makanya, an old woman known for her kind and peaceful ways. Sisiwe and Mother Makanya were grinding corn to make mealy-mush for the children one morning. When they heard the roar of the Great Lion they stiffened in fear despite themselves!

Sisiwe expressed herself in this way–

"Oh, Mother Makanya," Sisiwe said, "how much longer must we tremble at the sound of The Great Lion's roar?"

"It is not for us to say, my daughter Sisiwe," Mother Makanya smiled sadly and said, "our suffering and pain is the will of Olurun, the father of heaven. Only he can decide when it shall stop."

"Oh, I cannot believe that. I cannot believe that Olurun would be so cruel to his people."

Mother Makanya looked forlornly across the grassy savannah, fingering her robe.

"Sisiwe, my daughter, it its not for us to question the will of Olurun. Only to follow it, as best we know."

Sisiwe looked hard into the hot sun.

"I do not question Olurun, Mother Makanya. I only question why our people blame him for what we are doing to ourselves. It is because of our fear that we tremble at Sihkulumi's words. That is not the will of Olurun. We have become so afraid that we bow and scrape at the Great Lion's feet!"

"Daughter," Mother Makanya frowned gravely, "you should listen more often to the teachings of the priests Zitu and Utu. Perhaps then you would not become so angry. Their instruction would help you to better understand."

"I have listened to the teachings of priests Zitu and Utu," Sisiwe answered with fiery scorn, "I have also watched as their bellies grow fat." Sisiwe's eyes narrowed as she wagged a finger at Mother Makanya. "Why do they not starve as our children do? Answer me that! Themba says the food they eat comes straight from the table scraps of the Great Lion's table—"

"Sisiwe!" cried Mother Makanya. "What devil made you say that? Our priests are servants of Olurun, the father of heaven."

"I do not think so," replied Sisiwe. "I think they are servants of the Great Lion; and one more thing—"

Mother Makanya and Sisiwe went on arguing about the Great Lion. The heat waves from the sun pounded down upon them as they grew more and more upset.

The air shimmered in the distance as they beheld Themba wearily entering the village. The women stopped quarreling as they saw Themba coming across towards their grass hut. Themba raised his spear to greet them.

"Sakabona, Sisiwe, Mother Makanya." The tall, eagle-eyed Themba called out to them.

"Usaphila, Themba," the two women answered sweetly.

The pleasant expressions on their faces made it appear no quarrel was in progress.

"Have you brought us food, Themba?" asked Sisiwe hopefully.

Themba looked at the ground, because he was afraid to look Sisiwe in the eyes.

"No," he began, "the Great Lion is having a feast to honor himself. "He took for his party all the food I was bringing to you and the children."

"But Themba," said Sisiwe, disappointed. "Our children cry out in their hunger."

Themba knew this. At night he heard them crying in their sleep. He felt great sadness that because of the Great Lion, he could no longer feed his children. Once he was known as a proud and mighty hunter, but when the Great Lion came to rule, all that came to an end.

"There is still a little mealy-mush, isn't there?" asked Themba quietly. "The children may have my share, I am not hungry."

Sisiwe turned her face away and groaned.

"Mealy-mush. YUCK!"

"Mealy-mush is good for them, Sisiwe," Mother Makanya consoled her.

"Mealy-mush?" Sisiwe exclaimed in disbelief and dismay. "Mealy-mush! I feed them mealy-mush until they are about to become mealy-mush!" She looked at Themba with outrage and her eyes flashed with anger. "When will we have meat, Themba?"

Themba continued to look at the ground.

"I-I don't know, Sisiwe. We will have to wait, Sisiwe, we must have patience."

"But we have waited," replied Sisiwe. "I am tired of waiting, Themba."

"I also am tired, Sisiwe. I am very tired."

"We are all tired," Mother Makanya agreed.

"Well, you do not show it!" Sisiwe burst out at them.

"But honey-bird-" Themba began to plead.

"Don't you 'honey-bird' me, Themba! Don't you-don't you-speak to me until you bring my children food!"

"But honey-I-I mean, Sisiwe-" Themba stammered as Sisiwe waved a hand of dismissal in his face, "-please understand. I'm doing all that I can-"

"Oh, I think I will go cook some mealy-mush." Sisiwe casually commented and walked away with a shrug. "What mealy-mush there is left-"

Themba watched Sisiwe leave, her shoulders bowed in disgust, as she went into their grass hut alone. Mother Makanya was very concerned for Sisiwe. The old woman worried that nothing could be done to lift the spirits of Themba's wife.

About this time an old man came to greet Themba and Mother Makanya. This old man went here and there, clinging to a wooden staff. No one really seemed to know where he came from in the land. Some among the villagers whispered that this old man was known to have beheld and done much mischief. There were those who even believed he was really a magician. This old one was known as Grandsire Damasi.

"Sakabona, Mother Makanya. Ho-Themba!" The old man greeted them as he raised his wooden staff. "How are we today?"

"Usaphila, Grandsire Damasi." Themba and Mother Makanya murmured an answer.

"Eh? Eh? " The old man looked at them both. "What is the matter here? Why are we so sad now? Come! Out with it, the both of you."

Themba and Mother Makanya looked to each other to see who would tell it first.

"It is Sisiwe," sighed Themba. "I don't know how I can make her see that I am doing the best that I am able."

Mother Makanya smiled sadly and put her arm around Themba's shoulders.

"All we can do here," she said as she looked skyward, "is put our faith in Olurun, father of heaven."

The old man snorted and smiled a wry smile, wiping his nose with a scrap of cloth.

"Hmph, of course. That is good, sweet Mother. However, there may also be times when the mighty Olurun wishes us to help ourselves with the gifts he has given us. Hmmn, don't you think, Themba? The father of heaven, in his wisdom—no doubt, has given us many ways to end our sorrows."

Themba could recall having heard all this before.

"What ways, Grandsire," he asked in tired voice, "of what ways do you speak?"

There was a twinkle of mischief in the old man's eye.

"Ways beyond number, my son, ways beyond number. I am an old man and I have traveled far. Hee-hee, many times I have journeyed to the land beyond the hills."

Grandsire Damasi beckoned Themba to come to his side with a wrinkled, crooked finger. Themba nearly stepped forward, before Mother Makanya blocked him with her stout body.

"So what of it, old man?" Mother Makanya said with a suspicious frown. "You are known to have always put yourself in the middle of business not your own. Shoo! Don't trouble us with your schemes and trickery!"

Grandsire Damasi stumbled, but regained and held his ground leaning on his wooden staff.

He mumbled his disapproval and made an ugly face at Mother Makanya.

He nodded to Themba once more.

"Ack! You should be grateful that I have, for I and I alone, know the secret that will defeat the Great Lion Sihkulumi."

That sly smile glowed once more upon his lips.

Themba sighed to Mother Makanya. He did not believe the old man knew any secret.

"What is it this time, Grandsire? What is this secret you know? What must I do?" Themba folded his hands across his chest. "Are you going to give me a potion to take, or maybe a magic pill to swallow," Themba hefted his spear in the air and sighted an imaginary target, "a magic pill that will give me the strength to destroy-"

Mother Makanya raised her hands to her mouth to keep from screaming out that terrible thought that was the secret hope of all the villagers. Grandsire Damasi shook his head and wiped his nose again with his scrap of cloth. When he looked upon Themba again, his eyes gleamed with a special delight.

"Hmph, no, no, no, nothing like that, my son," the old man told him. "Do you not realize the power of the Great Lion? What it is that makes him so mighty and strong? Forgive me, my son, there is no special magic that will serve us here. You must use your own courage, cleverness and wisdom."

Mother Makanya grunted bitterly when she saw that Themba was beginning to believe the old man.

"Do not listen to him, Themba," she said, her mouth wrinkling like a prune. "That man tells many tales, but none are true. I warn you now for I must go and help Sisiwe. Remember Themba, Peace."

"Peace, Mother Makanya," the men both answered.

Themba and Grandsire Damasi waved goodbye. They watched with care as Mother Makanya walked through the shadows towards Sisiwe's hut.

When both were quite sure that she was inside the hut with Sisiwe, Themba turned eagerly once again to the old man. The old man chuckled, his eyes glittering with this new opportunity to share his knowledge.

"Now about the secret–" Themba began in a hushed whisper.

"Hee-hee, yes my son, the secret. You shall hear–you shall hear. First of all Themba, you must travel to the land beyond the hills. it is there that you will meet the three tests that must be overcome if you are to reach the Ivory Necklace of Wisdom. Eh? Got that?"

"Tests? Necklace?" Themba slowly shook his head. He did not understand. "What do these mean to me?" he asked. "How will they help me defeat Sihkulumi?"

The old man stooped low and grabbed a handful of sand. He let it spill loosely between his fingers and looked up at Themba. The old man shaded his eyes from the sun.

"Because it will be with the Necklace and only with the Necklace that you will know how to defeat Sihkulumi, the Great Lion."

Themba stood still in the shadow of the sun. He did not yet understand. Grandsire Damasi raised up to put his wrinkled hand on Themba's shoulder.

"You will see, my son, you will see. All your questions will be answered, but first you must attain the Necklace." Grandsire Damasi looked to his wooden staff. He rubbed his fingers over the rough, gnarled wood. After a moment, and with much sadness, he gave the staff to Themba. "Eh? Now here, put down your spear and take up my staff. I am an old man and have used it to the limit of my time. I can go no further than I have. Believe me when I say that you would do well to use it now, for I give to you the staff of truth. Eh? Close your eyes–tap it three times upon the ground, and it will take you anywhere you desire." Grandsire Damasi's eyes seemed to burst into flames. "It will take you to the land beyond the hills, to the three tests, and to the Ivory Necklace."

A sly smile came to the old man's lips once more.

"I leave you now, Themba. Now it is up to decide how you will choose to use the staff of truth. Eh? Peace Themba–"

"Peace, Grandsire Damasi." Themba muttered, almost lost in his own thoughts.

Themba was now all alone. He carefully studied the rugged staff he held in his two hands. He silently compared it to his spear that now lay on the sandy ground. How could a tool used for holding yourself upright be more important than a tool for hunting animals and catching meat?

"I wonder if it will work?" Themba asked himself. "–and if it does, what are the dangers I might find awaiting me? It may be safer to remain here and wait for our sorrow to end. Hmmnn, somehow, that does not seem quite right. Grandsire Damasi gave me this tool and I would do honor to him to find a use for it. There may well be some way I can bring an end to the pain and suffering of my family and my people with this staff, and that is at least worth a try."

Themba closed his eyes and raised the staff from the ground. He tapped it once, and the winds began to whistle and howl about the compound. He tapped it twice, and heard thunder as crackling lightning light up the sky and split the trunk of a nearby tree. He tapped it for a third time and to his surprise, felt the force of a hurricane carrying him away as spinning all around him he heard the rush of the wind and the cries of wild birds!

When the wind finally clamed down and Themba opened his eyes, he found he was picking himself up out of a grassy swamp. Somehow the hot day traded itself for cool night and the stars stared down on him like a thousand eyes in a black face. Themba could hear the crickets and frogs cry 'cheep-cheep' in the dark, and further beyond the soggy ground up into the trees growled and rumbled the voices of much bigger animals. Themba could not know where he was, but the way his hands trembled upon the glowing staff told him he was afraid.

Suddenly, Themba heard the hiss of a ferocious voice.

"YOU THERRREEEE!"

Themba whirled and saw a very tall woman floating above the wet grass before him. This woman was dressed in a long flowing bluish-black robe, and her skin was the greenish yellow color of a crocodile. There was an ugly mask made of tree bark shielding her face, and through the weave of her long black hair she wore a scarlet feather. The moon smiled and framed her head like a crown. She hovered closed to Themba, her voice coming to him in a slow hiss.

"I am the Lady of the Imamba Serpent, Guardian of the Scarlet Feather."

The floating woman told Themba this as she slowly raised her arms above her head. The wind seemed to be answering her summons, whisking through the grass and ruffling the folds of her dark robe. A terrified Themba cursed himself that he was armed with nothing but this old man's staff!

"Aaaahh! What is that noise?" cried Themba, as he looked with fear around him.

The woman behind the tree bark mask laughed coolly at Themba. The sound of her laughter made Themba feel like a little child. Themba could see the dancing flames of her playful, merry eyes. The woman lowered her arms and the winds skittering through the trees and along the puddles and ponds became still again.

"Why concern yourself? It is only my serpents and the wind in the grassssss," she hissed.

Themba now understood. The Lady of The Imamba Serpent was to be his first test. He made an effort to appear brave, and walked towards her until they were nearly face to face. He set the end of his staff against the wet grass.

"Now that you have told me who you are, I will tell you who I am. I-I am Themba, and I am looking for the Ivory Necklace of Wisdom so that I may defeat the Great Lion Sihkulumi."

The very leaves seemed to shake in the darkness when the Serpent Woman laughed this time.

She pointed a finger as sharp as a fang at Themba. He took a step backward in fright.

"You? Defeat Sihkulumi?? You who are frightened by the sound of my serpents and the wind in the grass? Surely you must be joking. Listen to me, Themba. You would do better to go back to the land where you were born. Run back to your children, Themba, and to your lonely little wife and hide behind her skirts. I am sure she can protect you. Run! Hide! Now, I say, now!

These words made Themba very angry as the Serpent Woman's laughter made echoes in the trees.

"I will not turn back," he told her. "I may be frightened easily, but I will fight as well as ever to protect my family."

The woman snarled at him from behind the mask. The bluish-black robe flapped in the wind about her like the wings of a vulture. She stabbed a finger into Themba's face once more.

"You fool! You will be less than a small mouthful for my serpents from the deep." The Lady of the Imamba Serpent began to chant, "Serpents, Serpents,
from the deep,
awaken from your sleep!
SERPENTS, SERPENTS,
from the deep,
Awaken from your sleep!"

She began to dance in the air around Themba, gliding in the night, singing her evil chant, her feet splashing in the wet grass. Now it seemed to Themba in his fear, that he could hear other voices in the night and feel the presence of snakelike shapes chanting with the Serpent Woman. These were the voices of the swamp and the pit, chanting with the Lady of the Imamba Serpent, as she wove her dance round and round Themba, blinding him and confusing him-

"SERPENTS, SERPENTS,
                    FROM THE DEEP
awaken from your sleep–
                    SERPENTS, SERPENTS,

                                                            FROM THE DEEP
                    AWAKEN FROM YOUR SLEEP–
SERPENTS, SERPENTS,
                    FROM THE DEEP
AWAKEN FROM YOUR SLEEP!!"

Themba could hear the hissing of a thousand poisonous vipers. He wanted to run, he wanted to hide, but did not even have the courage to take another step. The Lady of the Imamba Serpent continued to weave her dance around him, the voices continued to chant, and the hissing of the serpents grew so loud it was driving him mad with fear. Themba closed his eyes and waited for the serpents to come through the grass to wrap themselves about his body. He expected them to come out of the ground in the thousands, to bite and hiss and suck the very life and choke from him his final breath.

Themba stood still while the hissing became unbearable to his ears. The voices and the dancing continued, there were long shadows crisscrossing his body like living ropes. Themba expected the serpents at any moment to consume him, and yet, even though the hissing and voices and chanting and dancing continued, still, there were no serpents. Themba began to wonder as he shivered with fear. What if, he thought, there were no serpents?

He opened his eyes. What if everything the Lady of the Imamba Serpent told him was nothing more than a web of lies she was weaving?

Could it be possible that she was really only using his own fear against him? Yes! Surely that was so! That was it! Themba jumped high in the air and reached out. He seized the Lady of the Imamba Serpent by the wrist and snatched away her tree bark mask! All at once the hissing and the chanting stopped.

Themba looked the woman straight in the eyes.

"There are no serpents." Themba told her firmly.

Now it became very quiet in the swamp. Themba could see for the first time that now the Lady of the Imamba Serpent was afraid. The woman turned her eyes away from Themba. She took two quick steps backward, but Themba held her fast by the wrist.

"How did you ever guess? You are right. There are no serpents. There are only lies filled with evil. I was sure you would believe them, then your own fear would have destroyed you as it has so many others. Where did you find the courage to overcome my lies and thus defeat me? How could this have ever happened? I—" The Lady of the Imamba Serpent stared at Themba's staff, a question forming on her face and lips. "Oh—here," she plucked the Scarlet feather slowly and reluctantly from her hair. "The Scarlet Feather of Courage is yours. Now you are free to continue your journey."

"The Scarlet Feather of Courage." Themba repeated to himself thoughtfully.

The Lady of the Imamba Serpent handed Themba the feather. Themba took it and smiled, leaning on his staff and admiring it until he finally tucked it under his belt. The Serpent Woman turned silently to go, but Themba made her halt.

"Before you go, wait a moment," said Themba, "I was instructed I must face three tests. You have been only the first. Can you tell me what the second test might be?"

The Lady of the Imamba Serpent could barely conceal her bitterness and disgust.

"Ahhh, do not rejoice so soon." The Serpent Woman placed her tree bark mask back upon her face and stiffened once again with pride. "The second test is the Lord of the Wild Animals. You can take my word for it, you will not defeat him. He is stronger and more clever that you are. You would be wise not to walk in his land. I leave you with a warning, Themba-"

"You can keep your warnings for all they are worth," boasted Themba, "I won't be needing them. I will pass the other tests as easily as I have defeated you."

The Lady of the Imamba Serpent could barely conceal the scornful smile behind her mask. Now having defeated her, she would bet anything that Themba's overconfidence would be his undoing. He would find out too late that he was no match for the Lord of the Wild Animals.

"Very well, you fool," laughed the Lady of the Imamba Serpent as she hovered again on the wind, "find the way to your own defeat. Remember, I warned you; go no further if you value your life. All you will be choosing is your own loo-sssssing-"

The Serpent Woman spitefully rose on a gust of wind and was gone in a blink of an eye.

Themba stood in the middle of the swamp with his staff in his hands. He was full of pride and joy over having passed the first test. Now he began to think about what lay ahead for him.

"She said it was not wise to walk in the Land of the Wild Animals; that my life would be in danger," Themba muttered to himself, "-but I was once a mighty hunter, and still I am. I should be strong enough to defeat any cleverness. Besides, I cannot continue to let my children go hungry. I must go on-"

Themba closed his eyes and raised the staff from the ground. He tapped it once, and the winds began to howl. He tapped it twice and heard thunder in the sky. He tapped it for a third time and once again it seemed he was being carried away by a hurricane. All around him whirled the wind drumming against his ears and the cries of wild birds flapping their wings.

When the wind stopped and Themba opened his eyes, he found himself in a forest of oak trees.

This forest was very shady and the sun soaked light through the leaves above. There were ebony and mahogany trees here as well, and many flocks of different colored birds glided over the tops of them.

Themba was startled to hear a voice above him snarling, roaring and booming all at once.

"YOOOUUU THEEERRRREEE!"

Themba looked up just in time to see a very strange looking muscular man springing towards him from the top of a tall oak tree. The man spun head over heels and landed, feet first, in front of Themba.

This man was a strange sight. There were antelope antlers growing from the sides of his head. Cat whiskers growing from the sides of his nose. The muscles on his enormous arms were as big and hairy as any gorilla might flex before he cornered his prey. He possessed legs and feet that were gray and shaped like those of elephants. Over his huge chest he wore a leopard skin and a belt with many animals tails hanging over it.

Themba would have laughed but for the fear the man inspired in him. He watched carefully as the fellow paced around him, as though they were both wrestlers in the sand pit. The hairy man stroked his chin whiskers with a swagger.

"I am Lord of the Wild Animals," he said proudly, and his voice echoed throughout the entire forest. "I am Guardian of the Belt of WILDcat Tails." He folded his brawny arms across his chest. "All the wild animals bow down to me. WHO are you?"

Themba, who did not wish to be outdone, puffed out his chest. "Who am I? Ha-ha, surely you must be joking. Everyone knows who I am. Why I am Themba, conqueror of the Lady of the Imamba Serpent, possessor of the Scarlet Feather. Have you not heard the word? When I hunt, elephants climb to the top of trees in order to hide from me. I am looking for the Ivory Necklace."

Themba, convinced that the Lord of the Wild Animals was duly impressed, folded his own arms across his chest.

The Lord of the Wild Animals continued to stroke his whiskers thoughtfully.

"But before you reach the Ivory Necklace," he challenged, "you must first possess my belt of WILDcat tails!"

"Why is your belt of Wildcat Tails so important?"

The Lord of the Wild Animals walked around Themba as though he were searching for an opening to hurl him to the ground. He looked him over from head to toe as he began to crouch with his arms outspread.

"Your journey is long, Themba," said the Lord as he stroked his whiskers, "and filled with many dangers. I can end it for you here and save you many troubles. My belt of WILDcat Tails shows that I am Lord of All the Wild Animals and therefore their champion. I am forever protected from them and by them. The only way you can continue your journey is to pass through me. If you can defeat me in a test of -" The Lord smiled as he maneuvered around Themba, "-strength, I will give this belt to you."

"What will happen should you defeat me?"

The Lord of the Wild Animals laughed and Themba could see his front teeth were very long and very sharp. He clutched his staff and began to move towards a more open space.

"When I defeat you, I shall feed you to the wild animals, piece by piece, so that they may have their supper. Let us waste no more time with idle chatter. Stand ready!"

The two opponents circled each other slowly, each trying to find an opening in the other man's defense. Before Themba knew what was happening, the Lord of the Wild Animals seized Themba's staff in a lightning fast move.

Over and over again, he attempted to hurl Themba away while still holding onto the staff, but Themba clenched his teeth and held on even tighter. Scuffling in the forest clearing, the Lord of the Wild Animals flexed his mighty muscles and tossed Themba like a rag doll over his head! Themba landed somehow on his feet and found himself still holding onto the staff. The Lord of the Wild Animals looked with dismay into his empty hands. Themba spun and rushed him. He forced the Lord of the Wild Animals back with a mighty heave. The two struggled over the staff, each trying to force the other to the ground. Themba could feel a tingling power flowing somehow from the staff into his muscles, and to his surprise, the Lord of the Wild Animals was forced nearly halfway to the ground. The animals and the birds in the forest roared and screeched in protest.

"Ha! So you would feed me to the Wild Animals, would you now?" cried Themba. "Who will be served for supper now? You did not know you were fighting such a mighty hunter, did you now?" boasted Themba. "Soon I will teach you what true strength is all about–" Themba promised, as he continued to press the Lord inch by inch to the earthen floor.

"Argghhh!" cried out the Lord. "What Magic is this? How can this be? I am bigger, and my ferocious strength cannot be matched! How can this village hunter be winning? Now I must call upon the strength of all my kin. Spotted Leopard give me your strength! Mighty elephant give me your strength! All the Wild Animals of the field and the forest; GIVE YOUR STRENGTH TO ME!! WE MUST DESTROY THEMBA!!!!"

There was a tremendous roar throughout the whole forest. Themba could feel the very ground beneath his feet shiver and shake. Even the ants in the blades of grass seemed to nip at his heels. The bull elephants boomed out a chorus of approval as the Lord of the Wild Animals slowly began to force Themba to his knees.

Now the tables were turned and it was Themba who could not believe what was happening.

"I was a fool to be so overconfident," he told himself, "as to think I could defeat the Lord of Wild animals with strength alone. Whatever could have gotten into me? Now he has tricked me and I am the one with his knees nearly to the ground. Who could have expected he would use a strength more than his own? The strength of all the Wild animals is now pitted against me! What can I use as a weapon against this display of trickery?" Themba was almost knees to the ground when an idea struck him. "I have it!" Themba reached inside his belt. "The Scarlet Feather!" He brought the feather forth.

Themba began to tickle the Lord of the Wild Animals' nose with the feather.

The Lord began to snicker and then erupt into uncontrollable laughter. He swung this way and that at Themba with enormous paws to get him to stop, but Themba ducked and dodged and kept on tickling him. The Lord of the Wild Animals forgot himself and let go of Themba's staff.

Themba tickled him without mercy and he fell to the ground, kicking his legs at the sky. The Lord laughed so hard tears rolled down his cheeks and his whole body shook.

The Lord of the Wild Animals pointed his finger as he began to recover from the attack of laughter provoked by Themba.

"HA-hee-HA-you-you tricked me, Themba! Youuuu tricked me! This was supposed to be a contest of strength! You didn't win through strength. You won by-by-by-"

Themba stood over The Lord of the Wild Animals with his staff in one hand and the Scarlet Feather in the other. He waved away all other protests.

"What does it matter whether I won by cleverness instead of strength. The fact remains, I have won by bringing you to the ground. Now I am Lord of the Wild Animals. The Belt of Wildcat Tails is mine!"

"But-HA! But-but-HA-Hee! But-but-but-HA-HEE-ho! But-HA-HEE-HO-HA! Oh, here!"

The Lord took off the belt and threw it at Themba.

Themba tied the belt tightly around his waist and put the Scarlet feather back inside. All the animals of the forest and savannah came out into the clearing to witness the event. The Impala, the Cape Buffalo, The Gnu, The Rhinoceros, the Chimpanzee, the Aardvark, the Flamingo, the Mamba and Gorilla, among many, many others bowed low to the new Lord of the Animals. The defeated former Lord sat up, folded his arms and frowned.

"Thank you all for the honor." Themba bowed in return. "Now this has been the second of my my tests. Does anyone here have any idea what the third test will be?"

There was a silence through the forest that only the cry of a crow could pierce.

"No one has ever gotten this far," admitted the former Lord most glumly, "besides, even were I to have such knowledge I wouldn't share it with the likes of you! What are you waiting for now? You have the Belt of Wildcat Tails. You are now the Lord of the Wild Animals. The strength of these creatures is pledged to you. For any other mortal that would be enough. What need have you to pass any more tests?" The former Lord rose stiffly and shrugged his muscular, mighty arms. "Why hunt more than you need? I will say no more. I go now. The decision to go on must rest with you."

The former Lord of the Wild Animals bounded back into the tree tops and disappeared.

Themba stood alone, as all the animals returned to their favorite places in the forest. He held the staff in his hands and considered his next step. Why indeed was there any need to go on now?

"He is right," thought Themba, "this is not a journey meant for glory. Now that I am Lord of the Wild Animals, I could return with more than enough food for Sisiwe and my children. The entire village could become a land of plenty."

Themba heard a roar boom out from the forest and suddenly saw The Great Lion Sihkulumi in his mind's eye.

"I have forgotten the whole reason for my journey. No amount of plenty would stop the Great Lion from bringing terror and sorrow and misery to my people. No, food is not enough. We must be free of the Great Lion forever. This journey must continue. I must go on and meet the third test–"

Themba closed his eyes and raised his staff from the ground. He tapped it once, and the winds began to howl against his face. He tapped it twice, and angry gray clouds gathered and thundered overhead. One more time he tapped, and he was spun away as though lifted by the force of a hurricane! The lightning flashed and the rush of the wind uncovered groans of agony and cries of suffering among wild birds scattering to escape!

When the swirling colors of the wind stopped and Themba opened his eyes, he found himself on a high cliff, overlooking yellow plains and green mountains. The sun sat on the hilly throne of the horizon, and the clouds sailed by like flying carpets to the west. All among the plains and the mountains was quiet and still.

Themba sensed a presence nearby he could not yet see.

Now Themba heard a voice that hummed in the air and flowed like water. The voice was calm and steady. Themba felt it in his mind more than heard it with his ears.

"Who are you, sir, standing there?"

Themba turned in the direction of the voice. Over his shoulder, standing in front of a dark cave, was a man in a shimmering golden robe. The hair on his head was a white mane and around his neck were pieces of gleaming ivory.

"Who are you?" asked Themba.

The man smiled and his face glowed like the moon.

"I am the Emperor of the Great Plains, Guardian of the Ivory Necklace. I am the third and final test for those who seek the Ivory Necklace. Who are you?"

"I am Themba–"

"Ah, yes, the Spirits speak of your journey."

"I am Themba, conqueror of the Lady of the Imamba Serpent, sole possessor of the Scarlet Feather."

Themba showed him the feather with pride.

"You have proven therefore that you have courage. That is as it should be."

The Emperor of the Great Plains did not seem particularly impressed. Themba swallowed and almost timidly placed his hands on the belt around his waist.

"I am also victor over the Lord of the Wild Animals. Now I also possess the Belt of Wildcat Tails."

Themba thought that would convince this fellow who he was dealing with, but the Emperor only smiled.

"You have proven you can think and act with cleverness. That too, is as it should be."

What did this man want of him?

"I have come for the Ivory Necklace," Themba announced, as he lifted up his staff to defend himself. "I stand ready to fight!"

The Emperor laughed softly, and pushed away Themba's outstretched staff with a fingertip. He made his way over to perch on a small boulder. The Emperor regarded Themba with the eyes of an owl. He seemed to see right through to Themba's soul.

"Fight? No, Themba, we shall not fight here. There has been enough fighting. Now has come the time to think. I am not interested in your courage, Themba, you have already proven that. I am not interested in your cleverness, there are many animals on the plains who are clever, and besides, you have already proven that as well. No, Themba, I am interested in what you have learned."

This startled Themba as he brought his staff slowly to the ground.

"What I have learned?" he repeated, barely believing his ears.

"Yes, sit up here with me for awhile and enjoy the view."

Themba climbed up to flat spot atop the small boulder and sat beside the Emperor. The Great Plains stretched out below them all the way to the flaming red horizon. Themba looked into the Emperor's face. It was a face like rock aged a thousand years. Surely this man must know many things, thought Themba.

"Now what is it you want of me?" asked Themba, as he put his staff across his lap.

"Tell me this; what did you learn from your test with the Lady of the Imamba Serpent?"

"What did I learn?" Themba thought hard. "Well, I learned how important it is to overcome your fear. Your courage grows the more you fight for what is important to you."

"How did you feel once you knew in your soul that test was passed?"

"How did I feel? I felt-strong! Yes, very strong. But I became overconfident and thought I was stronger than I actually was."

The Emperor nodded thoughtfully as the shadows lengthened across the plains.

"I see. When did you know you were not as strong as you supposed yourself to be?"

"I was fighting with the Lord of the Wild Animals when it became clear to me my strength would not be enough."

"What did you learn from your test with him?"

Themba looked far away over the plains and tossed a pebble over the cliff. He heard it echoing as it skipped away down into the shadows. What was the need for all these questions?

"I learned that one must be able to think clearly in times of danger even when strength is not enough."

The Emperor again nodded thoughtfully.

"Now how does it feel to have passed that test?"

Themba frowned with irritation. What was this all about? One question after another! Sooner or later, the Emperor would ask him a question whose answer he did not know. After that, what would happen to him? Themba went on reluctantly just to be polite.

"I am not sure. I know now I have the courage to overcome my fear. I also know that now I am able to think clearly in times of great danger. Unfortunately, I am not sure that is enough."

Themba looked at the Emperor. The expression on the aged face of rock was unchanged. There was no emotion to be read upon his features. There was something in that face that commanded the kind of respect reserved for the most honored of elders. Themba squinted against the waning sun.

"Now I have a question for you, sir," Themba began, "what shall I learn from this test?"

Themba could see the last rays of the setting sun flicker away in his eyes. The Emperor smiled as shadow covered half his face. He got up from his perch on the boulder and walked over to the edge of the cliff. The Emperor turned once again to face Themba.

"That is really up to you, Themba. I would say it all depends on how you answer this riddle. Tell me: 'Why is a King like a Teacher?'"

"Why is a King like a Teacher?"

The Emperor nodded and smiled silently.

Themba walked to the edge of the cliff. He watched the sun as it sank behind the green mountains. The Emperor regarded him at a distance with owl eyes.

"Why is a King like a Teacher? ...a teacher has students...a king,...subjects... teacher...king... needs...will...servants..."

Themba sat down at the edge of the cliff and put his hand under his chin. What could be the answer? The moments seemed to pass away into forever. The darkness was gathering itself about Themba like a cloak.

Finally the Emperor turned to the dark cave behind him.

"Well, it seems you do not know." The Emperor started to walk back to his cave. "There is no dishonor in not knowing. Well, perhaps next time–"

"WAIT!" Suddenly it came to Themba! "Why is a King like a Teacher?" The Emperor halted in his step. "For a teacher...to teach well, she must know her children. She must be a servant to their needs. For a King...to rule wisely, he must know his subjects. He must serve their needs, be a servant to their will. Both must be servants to the people!"

The Emperor nodded with a measure of pleasure.

"Well done, my son. You have passed the test of wisdom." He took off the necklace and held it high in the air. The Emperor chanted a prayer in a language Themba could not understand. "Themba, the Ivory Necklace is now yours to use as you wish." He turned and placed it in carefully in Themba's hands.

Themba fingered the pieces of gleaming ivory and still a question formed upon his face.

"What I want to know is what power does it have? I asked Grandsire Damasi, and even he could not tell me!"

Themba thought he saw an expression on the Emperor's face that was almost amusement.

"Sometimes finding answers with your own thoughts can be harder than beating out a snake or wrestling a wild animal. What do you think, Themba?"

"What do I think?" asked Themba. "Why do you say that?"

"Because I would like to know. What power do you think the Ivory Necklace might possess?"

"I do not know. I suppose it might well depend on what use I can make of it."

"That was said well, my son. Do you think it might be more important what you do with it, and how you use it, than what power it has for you?"

Themba struggled with his thoughts for an answer the Emperor might accept. What amazed him was what an agony this thinking could be! He wondered whether it would ever get any less painful.

"Why do you say that? Why do you keep asking one question after another? I thought the time for riddles was done."

Themba thought the Emperor was close to breaking out in laughter. He seemed on the verge of asking yet another question, but thought the better of it.

"I told you, Themba. I ask questions because I want to know. I will tell you this; the necklace has great power-for good or for evil. It all depends upon who wears it, and, just like you said, what use the wearer puts to it."

"But why is that?"

The Emperor looked out over the yellow plains as they darkened into night.

"More questions, Themba? That is good. Questions can be good." The Emperor's owl eyes fixed on Themba as he approached. "Whoever wears the necklace is forced to look deep into his own heart and soul. If there is good in him, he will find the joy of Life, the bright light of the knowledge of Olurun, father of heaven. The soul of such a one will be filled with love, and for all times that one will know peace."

The sun was beneath the horizon now.

"What happens should there be great evil in the wearer's soul?" asked Themba.

The stars whirled in the sky and lit the face of the Emperor as he spoke this time.

"When the necklace reveals great evil in the wearer, then that one is forced to feel a pain that multiplies without end. That one will be forced to look into their heart and soul and find that every wickedness and every foul act has eaten away all the places where the soul can live. There will be no life in that one fit for even caterpillars. Every flaming devil within him will be set loose like fire ants, to weigh him down to drown in a river of molten lava and swarming red locusts.!"

Now it was night and darkness was spilled across all the plains. The Ivory Necklace still gleamed in Themba's hands. He clutched it between his fingers.

"This Ivory Necklace, then," said Themba quietly, "is the knowledge of good and evil."

"Yes, Themba, the knowledge of good and evil in everyone. Choose carefully who is to be the wearer. I leave you now, my son, to find the answers to your own questions. Peace, Themba."

"Peace, my friend."

Themba thought of one more question to ask, but as he turned in the direction of the dark cave, he discovered the Emperor of the Great Plains had disappeared.

Themba stood all alone on the high cliff. He held his staff in one hand, and the Ivory Necklace in the other. Themba was afraid to put it on, because he did not know how much good or how much evil there was to be found in him. Whatever the case may be, he knew he needed to find out before he returned to his people.

Themba slowly and with great reluctance put the gleaming pieces of ivory around his neck.

All at once his soul began to churn and burn with fire. The growing inner pain made him grip his staff and he fell to his knees in a gasp of agony. The sorrows and regrets of his life ate away at him like beetles. The weight of all that he had done that Olurun would not approve of became nearly intolerable. Slowly, just as he began to think he could bear it no more, the fire in his soul began to fade. It became less and less hot, cooled and finally did not burn at all.

Themba's soul became calm and his face filled with happiness. It was as the Emperor told him. Now he knew the good inside him was greater than the evil. Now Themba knew the truth. He could return to his people and help them with this new knowledge.

Themba closed his eyes and raised his staff from the ground. He tapped it once, and the winds were the cries and howls of spotted hyenas. He tapped the staff twice, and heard the flocks of birds that the sound of the thunder chased away. He tapped it three times, and the ground shook and quivered all around him. The rush of the wind drowned out everything except the trumpeting sounds of the elephants-

When Themba opened his eyes, he found himself once again in his own village. Grandsire Damasi was the first to greet him.

"Themba, you returned," exclaimed the old one, "and you have the Ivory Necklace. The Great Lion becomes more evil with every moment. The people cry out in pain, he causes so much suffering amongst the children. He must be destroyed, Themba! You must kill him!"

There were others in the village who agreed with Grandsire Damasi.

"Kill him Themba," they pleaded, "we can wait no longer–"

"RRRROOOOOAAAARRRR!!!"

The Great Lion came into the village, followed by Priests Zitu and Utu, and the throng of people scurried away. The Great Lion was dressed in long, flowing red robes and a gold crown sat upon his brow. Each one of his teeth were large and white and shiny. They were as sharp as the tips of spears. The Great Lion's face was like a mask of deadly rage and anger.

"Now you have finally returned, have you, Themba?" The Great Lion snarled. "Be careful you do not anger me, or I'll take your children and eat them for my breakfast!"

The Great Lion licked his lips and smacked his chops. He smiled with wicked pleasure.

Sisiwe and Mother Makanya came running from their huts.

Themba, I am glad you returned," said Sisiwe breathlessly, "did you bring us food?"

"Themba," said Mother Makanya sadly, "we are without hope. You must join us to pray to Olurun for help."

"SILENCE!" ordered the Great Lion. "Silence, or I'll rip out your guts and grind them for my bread. Get back to you places! Back I say! Themba, aren't you forgetting something? Where is your offering to the Great Lion? Where is my gift, Themba, that I might spare your miserable life?!"

The villagers all peeked from behind the flaps in their huts with fright.

"Kill him, Themba!" cried Grandsire Damasi.

"The food, Themba!" pleaded Sisiwe.

"Pray with us, Themba!" demanded Mother Makanya.

"My gift, Themba!" commanded the Great Lion with a deafening angry growl.

Now Themba was truly confused.

"How can I answer all these needs? How can I be a servant to all of them?" Themba asked himself, as he fingered the Ivory Necklace in his hands. "I must have the wisdom to know how I must serve."

Something dawned in Themba's mind and he slowly removed the Ivory Necklace from about his neck. The beginning of an idea came to him. He bowed low to the Great Lion.

"Oh yes, O Great Lion Sihkulumi, I do have a gift for you, one that will give you the power to see deep into your heart, your very soul—"

The necklace sparkled in Themba's hands.

The Great Lion grinned devilishly at the offering.

"Very good, Themba, you know what's good for you and all the villagers. Yes, I have always wanted to see myself more completely. After all, am I not more beautiful than anything you can imagine?"

There was a fearful silence and no one said anything.

"AM I NOT BEAUTIFUL?" The Great Lion demanded with an angry roar.

Priests Zitu and Utu led all the villagers in bowing and scraping.

"Oh yes, oh yes, oh great and mighty lion!" The priests chanted, "You are beautiful, and we are UGLY!"

"See? I have taught them well. I AM BEAUTIFUL! This necklace that Themba has now brought me will allow me to see just how beautiful I really am. Hand it over, Themba—"

The Great Lion took the necklace from Themba's hands. Themba bowed again obediently.

"Yes, I like it," The Great Lion said, as the Priests put the gift about his neck. Utu brought forth a mirror so that the Great Lion could better admire himself. "Yes, the Ivory Necklace is a perfect fit for me—"

"So you have become a servant to Sihkulumi too." said Sisiwe with disgust. "So now you will join Zitu and Utu in bowing and scraping at his feet." Her eyes became heavy with tears. "You are a jackass penguin, Themba, and there is no more honor in being your wife!"

"Themba!" cried out Grandsire Damasi with anger. "What has happened to you? What have you done? Eh? You were the last hope to rid our village of this evilness. Now all hope is lost because you are too cowardly to kill this monster. Themba! You are a warrior no more!"

The hate in Grandsire Damasi's eyes as he walked away surprised even Themba.

Even the gentle and kind Mother Makanya voiced her dismay and disapproval.

"Olurun, the father of heaven, has turned his face away from you, Themba," she said. "You have lost your faith, you have deserted us! Now we will all perish!"

The people in the village agreed with her. Mother Makanya joined with Sisiwe, and all began to wail and sob-

"We disown you, Themba," rose up the cry of the people, "we disown you!"

Grandsire Damasi suddenly came back with Themba's spear. This was a shock to everyone.

He was bursting with the built up rage of all his years. The outrage spilled out of him and he could wait no longer. He faced the Great Lion on withered, spindly legs.

"Our people scream in pain because of your evilness. Now they will no longer!"

Grandsire Damasi lept up with a great cry. He charged the Great Lion with Themba's own spear. That was the moment Themba caught the old one's arm as the Great Lion's deadly roar resounded throughout all the village. He whirled Grandsire Damasi back out of death's way and into the horrified arms of Mother Makanya and Sisiwe.

"STAY BACK, GRANDSIRE!" ordered Themba. "LOOK!"

The people in the village could not believe their eyes. The Great Lion was doubling over and his face was filled with pain.

"Look," repeated Themba, "The Ivory Necklace is forcing the Great Lion to behold his own wickedness. LOOK!"

The Great Lion screamed as the pain seemed to multiply without end.

"OOOOOHHHHH-AAAAGGGGHHHHH!!! MY SOUL! MY SOUL! WHERE IS MY SOUL? MY SOUL IS GONE!!!!!" he cried helplessly, as he slowly sank to his knees. "AHHHH- THE FIRE ANTS-THE FIRE ANTS ARE IN MY BRAIN-MY VERY BONES!!!"

The flames in the Great Lion's brain and bones grew as hot as the molten lava from an exploding volcano.

"STOP THEM!" The Great Lion screamed. "THE FLIES AND THE ANTS ARE SETTING ME ON FIRE!!!"

The Great Lion attempted to claw the Ivory Necklace from his neck, but it shocked and burned his fingers. He rolled in agony on the ground. The villagers were stunned beyond belief.

"HOW CAN THIS BE? MY BEAUTY HAS BECOME UGLINESS! MY MIGHT HAS EVAPORATED FROM ME. The Great Lion whined as he pounded his head with his fists. "I STOOD ON THE BACKS OF THESE PEOPLE! WHO IN THIS VILLAGE DID NOT BOW AND GROVEL TO OBEY MY EVERY COMMAND? AAAARRGGGHHHH! ALL WAS GOOD! AAAAAA! NOW ALL IS EEEE-VIL! I ? AM EVIL???? I AM FILLED WITH EVVVILLL!!!"

"Take off your crown, defeated one." Themba commanded. "I, Themba, have returned to tell you what the entire village has prayed to hear. You are King no longer!"

The village people gasped with surprise. The light of victory shone in Themba's eyes.

"The necklace you now wear," Themba continued, "will prevent you from ever harming another living soul. Your brain will burn for every evil thought you have, and for every vicious act you attempt to commit your flesh will rot.

There was the scent of freedom in the air and the people began a low chant that grew louder and swelled as Themba spoke. Sisiwe chanted, Mother Makanya chanted, Grandsire Damasi chanted, and the entire village chanted with them. There seemed to be a great weight lifting from the backs of the people.

"Tell him, Themba, Tell him,
    Tell him, Themba, tell him,
        Tell him, Themba, tell him,"

And Themba told him.

"You can torture our people no longer. Our children will feed at your table. Our women will no longer tremble at the sound of your voice. Instead, I command you to return to the land from whence you came. The ugly sight of you will never be seen here again. Now that you have seen yourself as you really are, consider well what brought you low." Themba pointed his finger to the land beyond the hills. "GO!"

The once mighty and great lion crawled, broken and whimpering out of the village, never to be seen again. The people cried to the top of their lungs with great joy!

"THEMBA, our king!
    THEMBA, OUR king!!
        THEMBA, OUR KING!!!"

Sisiwe picked up the crown that lay carelessly in the dust.

"The crown is yours for the taking, Themba." said Sisiwe.

Themba held it for a moment and nodded to himself with a smile.

"This is not for me, Sisiwe. No one should ever wear this hideous crown again. The crown belongs to the people for their prayers. Now the people must be King."

"We want you to rule us," said Priests Zitu and Utu.

The priests began to bow low, but Themba stopped them.

"Please, all of you. If you would have me lead," he told them, "then I will lead without a crown. Let the people know me as a servant to their will."

Sisiwe shook her head and frowned her disapproval.

"Hmph. Really, Themba. Just think of all the diamonds and rubies and emeralds we could have once you made yourself King. Themba, I really don't see—"

"Tula!" commanded Themba. "By my side, woman."

Sisiwe's mouth fell open in dismay. Themba was known as a mighty hunter the last time he spoke to her like that. She looked nervously to Mother Makanya for help, but the old woman only smiled.

"I think I heard your man calling you, didn't I?" asked Mother Makanya.

Sisiwe turned to Grandsire Damasi. The old man's face glowed with that sly smile.

"Hee-hee, our mighty leader summons you, Sisiwe."

Finally, she turned back to Themba. He held out his hand to her patiently. She place her hand in his own and they stood together to the approval of the entire village.

"Now you must tell us, Themba," asked Priests Zitu and Utu. "What are we to do now that the Great Lion is no more our King."

Themba put his hand to his chin.

"Well," he looked to Priests Zitu and Utu, "what do you think we should do?"

The priests were stunned and looked nervously to each other.

"Why would you ask such a thing of us?" demanded the Priests.

"Because I would like to know what you think. You might have some good ideas the entire village could use." Themba looked around at the people in the village. "When I have heard every-one's ideas we will begin to make new plans," he announced, "new plans–"

"For a mighty empire, Themba." said Grandsire Damasi.

"–and a beautiful empire, Grandsire Damasi." added Themba.

"We must sing our praises to Olurun, the father of heaven!" cried Mother Makanya.

"We must dance the warriors' dance of freedom!" cried Grandsire Damasi.

"We must shout our sacred song of love!" Sisiwe declared.

Themba slowly raised the staff of truth to the sky as the stars twinkled.

"We will sing our praises to Olurun, the father of heaven.

We will dance the warriors' dance of freedom," proudly announced Themba, "and shout our sacred song of love, in this our mighty and beautiful empire. Let the drums speak and the celebrations begin!"

The rumble of Bala's Talking Drum brought us slowly back out of The Great Time. Bala gave thanks to Olurun in this way Brothers and sisters, as we return from The Great Time by the will and the grace of Olurun, the father of heaven. We thank him now with the songs of our praise, the dance of our freedom and the shouts of our love. Even more than this, we will thank him with the spirit of our peace in this our beautiful empire!

Olurun! We give thanks to thee! We will dance until the moon is crying tears of happiness! We chant our songs of love until the very trees themselves tremble with our rejoicing!

Bless us, O Mighty Olurun! Grant us a peace of wisdom that never ends!

And that was the entire story as Bala would tell it.

There are voices that do not come from your mother and your father. There are voices that do not come from your sisters and brothers, or your friends and neighbors. There are voices that do not come from human tongues. There are voices everywhere, speaking in the land. The voices of our ancestors, the voices of the Water People, the voices of our gods and heroes, speak and our heard by us when we choose to listen.

Olurun, the father of heaven, would have it so.

We tell and listen to the stories of our gods and heroes. We tell and listen to the stories of hardship and great struggle. We tell and listen to the stories where the journey for wisdom and courage and strength flows like the neverending river Sankuru and finally brings us home.

What Bala understood, he taught to us by word of mouth. He taught us to hear the voices others could not hear or understand by themselves. So that they would never be forgotten, he passed on the stories and great deeds of our people to all those would hear and speak. Through our voices, the voices of our greatest village heroes and mightiest spirits will live forever. We stand ready to open for all the invisible door to The Great Time.

Forever will it be so.

THE END

Printed in the United States
By Bookmasters